Food Groups

Grains

Lola Schaefer

Heinemann
LIBRARY

www.heinemann.co.uk/library

Visit our website to find out more information about Heinemann Library books.

To order:
☎ Phone 44 (0) 1865 888066
🖹 Send a fax to 44 (0) 1865 314091
🖥 Visit the Heinemann Bookshop at www.heinemann.co.uk/library to browse our catalogue and order online.

First published in Great Britain by Heinemann Library, Halley Court, Jordan Hill, Oxford OX2 8EJ, part of Harcourt Education. Heinemann is a registered trademark of Harcourt Education Ltd.

© Harcourt Education Ltd 2008
The moral right of the proprietor has been asserted.

Editorial: Diyan Leake and Kristen Truhlar
Design: Joanna Hinton-Malivoire
Picture research: Melissa Allison
Artwork: Big Top
Production: Duncan Gilbert
Originated by Modern Age
Printed and bound in China by South China Printing Co. Ltd.

ISBN 978 0 431 01517 0
12 11 10 09 08
10 9 8 7 6 5 4 3 2 1

British Library Cataloguing in Publication Data
Schaefer, Lola M., 1950-
   Grains. - (Food groups)
   1. Grain - Juvenile literature 2. Grain in human nutrition - Juvenile literature 3. Cookery (Cereals) - Juvenile literature
   I. Title
   641.3'31

Acknowledgements
The publishers would like to thank the following for permission to reproduce photographs: © Corbis p. **7** (Dung Vo Trung); © Dreamstime.com p. **10** (barley, Ejla; corn, Dannyphoto80; oats, Emielcia; rice, Jameshearn; wheat, Kovalvs); © Harcourt Education Ltd pp. **4** (MM Studios), **11** (Tudor Photography), **15** (Tudor Photography), **16** (Tudor Photography), **18** (Tudor Photography), **19** (Tudor Photography), **20** (Tudor Photography), **22** (MM Studios), **26** (Tudor Photography); istockphoto.com pp. **14** (Michael Valdez), **25** (Kurt Holter); © Masterfile pp. **17, 27** (Dan Lim); © Photodisc p. **9**; © Photolibrary pp. **6** (Anthony Blake), **8** (Anthony Blake), **12** (BananaStock) **13** (Anthony Blake), **21** (Foodpix), **23** (Foodpix), **24** (Stockbyte), **29** (Photononstop); © Punchstock p. **28** (BlueMoon Stock).

Cover photograph reproduced with permission © Masterfile (G. Bliss).

Contents

What are grains? 4

Where grains come from 6

Making grains into food 8

How grains look 10

How grains taste 12

Why grains are healthy 14

How many grains do you need? 16

Grains to eat for breakfast 18

Grains to eat for lunch 20

Grains to eat for dinner 22

Grains to eat for snacks 24

Keeping grains fresh 26

Do grains alone keep you healthy? 28

Glossary 30

Find out more 31

Index 32

Some words are shown in bold, **like this**. You can find out what they mean by looking in the glossary.

What are grains?

Grains are the seeds of some plants. Wheat, rice, and corn are three different grains. People all over the world eat grains in bread, crackers, noodles, and pancakes.

There are many different kinds of foods made with grains.

Each colour on this plate is for one of the five food groups.

Grains are one of the **food groups**. You need to eat grains each day as part of a good **diet**. Grains help your body stay healthy.

Where grains come from

Farmers plant seeds of grain in fields. The plants grow until they are **ripe**. Some farmers pick the ripe grains with large machines. Other farmers pick grains by hand.

Around the world, people eat more rice than any other grain.

This wheat flour will be sold in grocery stores.

The picked grains are taken to a place called a mill. Machines take the **kernels**, or seeds, from the plant. Some grain is ground to make **flour** or **meal**.

Making grains into food

Many foods can be made with **flours**. Bakers add water and other foods to flours. They make breads, cookies, cakes, or bagels.

A baker works with many different kinds of grains.

Onions and vegetables add flavour to rice.

Other grains, like oats and rice, are sometimes cooked in water or milk. The grains soften when cooked. People add **seasonings** to the grains and eat them.

How grains look

Many grains look alike. The **kernels** are smaller than the end of your fingernail. Each grain is longer than it is wide.

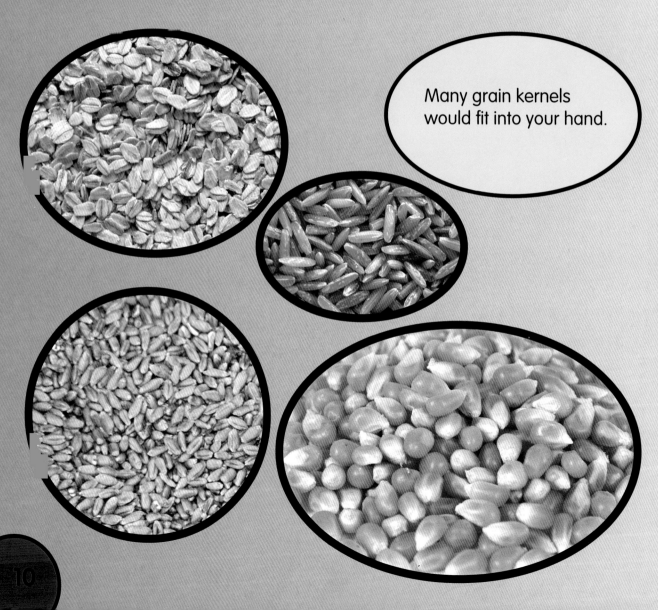

Many grain kernels would fit into your hand.

Corn kernels are small and almost round. They can be made into many things, such as these corn chips.

Most corn is yellow or white. Wheat is light brown. Rice can be black, brown, yellow, or white. Other grains are light brown or tan.

How grains taste

Many grains taste nutty. Some breads are made with the whole grain **kernel**. Those breads take longer to chew and have more flavour.

A ham sandwich made with whole grain bread is a healthy and tasty lunch.

Porridge is made from oats.

Most grains are cooked or baked before you eat them. Cooking makes the grains softer and easier to chew. Oats stay thick and chewy even after they have been cooked.

Why grains are healthy

Grains are full of **vitamins**, **minerals**, and **carbohydrates**. Your body uses carbohydrates to make **energy** for work or play. Vitamins and minerals help keep your body healthy and strong.

The carbohydrates in pancakes help your body make energy.

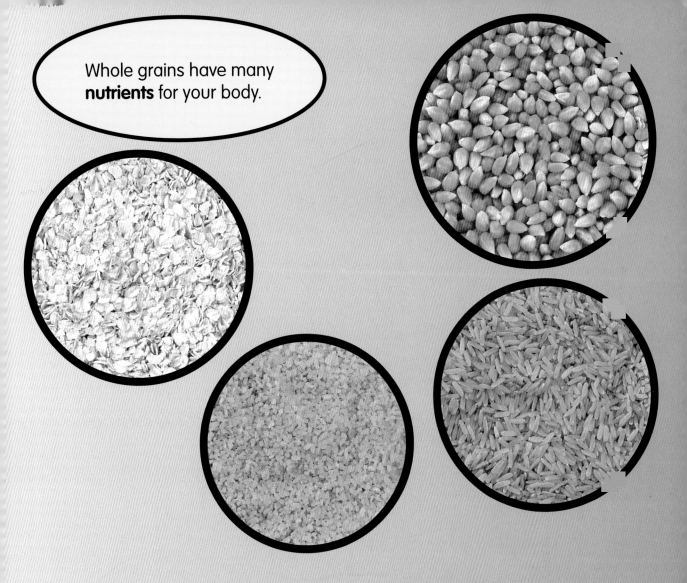

Whole grains have many **nutrients** for your body.

Whole grains that are made with the whole **kernel** are healthier. They have more carbohydrates and more **fibre**. Fibre helps your body use the vitamins and minerals it takes in.

How many grains do you need?

Most children 5–10 years old need 4–5 servings of grains each day. A serving could be a piece of toast or a portion of rice. It could be a bowl of pasta or a slice of pizza.

Each of these servings gives your body **nutrients** it needs.

Eat many different grains each day to stay healthy.

You should eat at least one serving of grains with each meal. Look for food labels that say "whole grain". These are the healthiest grains for your body.

Grains to eat for breakfast

Many breakfast foods are made with grains. A bowl of muesli, porridge, or cornflakes makes a good breakfast. Pancakes, waffles, toast, and bagels are also made with grains.

Try eating a bagel with one of these different toppings for breakfast.

Crunchy bites

Please ask an adult to help you.

- Stir the porridge oats and powdered milk together.
- Add the rest of the ingredients and mix well.
- Roll into 2.5 cm (1 in.) balls and place in the refrigerator for 2 hours.
- Serve and enjoy.

You will need:
- 175 grams porridge oats
- 175 grams powdered milk
- 125 grams crunchy peanut butter
- 125 grams honey
- 1 teaspoon of vanilla
- 60 grams raisins

Eat three or four crunchy bites for a healthy breakfast.

19

Grains to eat for dinner

Many people like to eat pasta for dinner. There are many different shapes of pasta to try. Maybe you like spaghetti, macaroni, or lasagna.

Whole grain pasta has a darker colour and more flavour.

Couscous is made from ground wheat.

Couscous is another grain people eat for dinner. Sometimes people eat it with meat or vegetables, or they make a salad with it. Rice is also a very popular food for dinner.

Grains to eat for snacks

Popcorn is the whole **kernel** of corn heated until it bursts open. Breadsticks and sesame sticks are also crunchy snack foods. When you need a snack, try one of these.

Popcorn is a fun, healthy snack to eat.

Snap and crack snack

- Place the cereal and snacks in a bowl.
- Add the peanuts and walnuts.
- Mix everything together.
- Divide into sealed bags.
- Take a bag with you to enjoy a snack on the go.

You will need:
- 250 grams of a healthy cereal
- 250 grams of a snack such as small pretzels
- 125 grams peanuts
- 125 grams walnuts

This snack will give you **energy** and **fibre**.

Keeping grains fresh

Grains like rice, oats, wheat, or barley need to be stored in air-tight containers. They will keep well in a cool, dry space. They should be stored out of the sunlight.

It is good to store grains in plastic containers.

Wheat flour can be used to make bread soon after it has been bought.

Whole grains spoil quicker than other grains. Use these grains as soon as you can. Place them towards the front of your cupboard.

Do grains alone keep you healthy?

Grains are good for your body. But you need more than grains to stay healthy. Eat foods from each of the other **food groups** and drink plenty of water.

Foods from different food groups can be served together to make a good meal.

Your body rests and repairs itself while you sleep.

As well as eating healthy foods, your body needs regular **exercise**. You should try and get a little each day. You also need to get plenty of sleep each night. Sleep helps you stay strong and well.

Glossary

carbohydrate part of food (such as bread or rice) that gives a person energy

diet what a person usually eats and drinks

energy power needed for a body to work and stay alive

exercise physical activity that helps keep a body healthy and fit

fibre rough part of food that is not digested. Fibre helps carry food through the body.

flour grain, such as wheat, that is ground up and can be used for cooking or baking

food group foods that have the same kind of nutrients. There are five main food groups, plus oils.

kernel grain or seed of a type of plant

meal ground grain that is larger than flour. People make foods with cornmeal.

mineral nutrient needed to make the body work correctly

nutrient substance (such as a vitamin, mineral, or protein) that the body needs to stay healthy and grow

ripe fully grown and ready to pick or eat

seasoning ingredient used to add flavour to food. Salt and pepper are two seasonings.

spelt one of the first grains to be grown by early farmers. It has a nutty flavour, has more protein than wheat, and is high in fibre.

tortilla flat, thin cake made from cornmeal or wheat flour

vitamin nutrient in food that the body needs to stay healthy. Nutrients help the body work correctly.

Find out more

Books to read

Go Facts: Healthy Eating, Paul McEvoy (A & C Black, 2005)

Look After Yourself: Eat Healthy Food!, Angela Royston (Heinemann Library, 2004)

What's on Your Plate? Breakfast, Ted and Lola Schaefer (Raintree, 2006)

Websites to visit

www.5aday.nhs.uk
Click on "Fun & Games" and then "Did You Know?" to find out amazing food facts.

www.childrenfirst.nhs.uk/kids/health/eat_smart/food_science/index.html
Click on the carbohydrates on the tray to find out more about why these are good for you and how many you need to eat each day.

www.nutrition.org.uk
Click on "Cook Club" for some great recipe ideas.

Index

barley 26
breakfast 18, 19
carbohydrate 14, 15
corn 4, 11, 18, 24
diet 5, 28
energy 14, 25
dinner 22
food group 5, 28
food pyramid 5
fibre 15, 25
flour 7, 8
kernel 7, 10, 11, 12,
    15, 24
lunch 20, 21
meal 7
mill 7

mineral 14, 25
nutrient 15, 16
plant 4, 6, 7
porridge 13, 18, 19, 20
rice 4, 6, 9, 11, 16,
    23, 26
rye 20
seed 4, 6, 7
snack 24, 25
spelt 20
vitamin 14, 15
water 8, 9, 28
wheat 4, 7, 11, 20, 26
whole grain 12, 15, 17,
    21, 22, 27